HIGH TICKET

Luigi Padovesi

Summary

CONQUERING SUCCESS 4

How to increase profits 4
Stand out from the competition 11
Plan your time 19
Set up the business plan 27
Business Manager 34
Accept failure 38
The importance of language 44
Plan for success 47

BRAND POSITIONING 52

Getting the customer to desire you 57
Create your own reputation 64

PROMOTE YOUR PRODUCT 67

PRICING 77

KNOW YOUR CUSTOMER 83

ERRORS TO AVOID 90

DIFFERENTIATE PRICES 90

DISCOUNTS 94

DO YOU NEED MONEY? 103

Conquering success

How to increase profits

Before understanding how to increase profits, we need to dwell on the various terms and have a clear idea of the terminology in this area. Revenue, revenues, profits, seem the same thing, but it's not like that at all.

Who does not know specifically the meaning of these words could make a mistake in using them inappropriately: let's clarify immediately these aspects.

Revenue is everything that enters the coffers of the company, regardless of expenses. So a company could be at a loss even with revenue from millionaires.

The revenue is instead the total revenue of the company: it is clear that a company started for tens of years will have obtained more money than one just started, but could still have a lower monthly profit.

The two concepts are not equivalent: while the revenue is a figure that does not depend on time, the profit (or profit) is defined in a precise period, usually monthly or yearly.

Finally, profit is the difference between the sum of each income and each expense (Profit = Revenue - Expenses).

But how can profits be increased?

Let's start with the basics: all companies aim to solve a problem for someone. Very often this aspect is not even clear to the entrepreneur, who has never clearly defined what kind of problem he is solving and who his ideal client is.

We are therefore often focused on the idea of recovering as many customers as possible, but losing the focus on our target:

a type of customer that already needs us and is looking for us, which would be enough to make a proposal to conclude the sale.

Consequently, the first thing to do, to use a successful marketing strategy is to know who you are targeting. After having identified the appropriate customers, as mentioned above, it is very important to use the appropriate message for each situation, which will serve to communicate that your product or service can satisfy certain needs and therefore be able to solve problems; all this can only be done through a clear and direct language, which is able to make immediately clear and unambiguous what is being proposed to the customer.

We should start using messages and concepts that make us understand immediately that our product or service can immediately solve a problem for the consumer: "From today when you have to buy a product, enter our site always active and buy now just one click!" We must not complicate our lives, we must give the impression that those who buy from us do it simply, quickly and clearly. A very important way to be able to best adopt the things said so far are social networks, through advertising. Through social networks, your business can spread its messages to a greater number of potential customers, quickly and with lower costs. The important thing, however, is knowing when to propose a certain product or service to the public, because if we choose a wrong moment or period, we risk not selling anything or selling very little.

The most appropriate things to do are, therefore:
- Create a message with an irresistible offer.
- Attract potential customers.

- Get publicity using an appropriate medium at the right time.

Stand out from the competition

Nowadays, organizations are increasingly struggling to differentiate themselves within an already complete market. Whether you work in any type of business or organization, the need to positively and appropriately distinguish your products or services from the competition is very important.

Improving service management is the most assured method for finding more importance in the eyes of customers.

This allows companies to adapt their products or services based on specific customer needs and requirements, favoring the trust rate through a more reliable level of support and services. Before talking about how to differentiate and offer a better product or service, one must understand that the worst companies ignore their competition.

But what is the competition?

All the commercial enterprises suffer the competition, it occurs when several economic subjects present in the market want to satisfy the same need for goods or services.

The purpose of businesses is to attract as many customers as possible. It is practically

a "race" for those who make the best product and those who are most successful.
On the market, apart from rare exceptions, we will find a very large number of companies competing with us to offer a similar service; there are no obstacles at the beginning when entering the market, since the product or service of a better activity, which better satisfies the customer, will certainly have more success than another which is the opposite since the consumer is absolutely free to choose.

Before thinking about how to "break down" the competition, we need to see what our strengths are; most of the times, it is not at all easy to understand which are the points of view that should be changed or improved, because some properties, which present us better than the competition, seem obvious and banal, while it seems to us much easier to describe one's points weak.

Most of the time it is useful to see ourselves through the eyes of others.

Almost always for us our qualities are non-existent, precisely because they are so natural that they seem banal and taken for granted: a simple way to bring up the truth about our qualities is simply to ask those around us.

After understanding their potential, the time has come to "study" competition through various points, including:

- Identifying competitors (understanding who is competing with us and with which tools).
- Understand the competition strategies and how they offer a better product or service than ours.
- Identify the strengths and weaknesses of the competition.
- Understand the level of competition ("if I try to do something to try to offer a better product or service than they do, will they do something?").

• Plan a means of improving your business to overcome competition.

Competition can be of various types, including:

❖ Product or service competition, ie those who offer products or services that are similar or lower in price.

❖ Generic competition, ie companies that sell products or services that belong to different categories but can be replaced.

❖ Competition at class level, ie those who offer products that belong to the same object category, but in a different variety.

❖ Budget competition, or those competing to appropriate a portion of the expenditure made by the consumer.

The main concept to be more successful than others is to sell a quality product at a low price in a short time.

We must understand that, however, there are many competitors and they have many resources available, it is not always so obvious to sell and be more successful than others, since they too are people like us who have the same goal and therefore will surely do something to pull themselves up once we have implemented our plans.

Plan your time

Have you ever wondered how you are spending your time?

Many argue that time is one of the most important factors and is considered essential and not to be underestimated and that often determines the success or the opposite in professional, family or personal life.

It is practically an indispensable and irreplaceable resource.

Good time management is essential to identify a high level of "personal effectiveness". Our mind works almost like a computer, when many incomplete or halfway ideas are presented to you, it is as if we had a large number of windows open on the computer at the same time, the performance falls a lot and consequently much of the work to be done will become slower, as well as time management.

This feeling of "not having control of what we are doing" and especially of our time, is the main source of anxiety, stress, and frustration.

In simpler words, the lack of time dramatically increases stress and anxiety, so it's how we organize ourselves during a day that can make the difference. Complaining about the little time available and the many things that need to be done certainly does not solve the problem.

When you have the idea that you no longer have a shred of time, it is because, in fact, we are the goals of someone else, so we should think about what we really want. Everyone is constantly busy solving problems, but few are aware of the opportunities already present that are offered to us every day, of their own well-being and above all of their future and of the projects we could implement.
A very large part of professionals or entrepreneurs at high levels live by

deadlines and many unexpected events. They use their time daily to solve unexpected and immediate problems. Very few people in the world are aware of this, planning safe goals for the future.

The time where it takes place and that's it, it's over, now it's time to stop and think, reflect and plan innovative and profitable strategies and finally make this a real reality. Reflecting and realizing these objectives, understanding and understanding the various techniques for managing one's own time means expressing and above all having the perfect control of one's life, not only professional.

All successful people understand what they want to achieve and how to do it, and especially how quickly they want to get it. They know how to distinguish important things from superfluous things, constantly choosing based on the time available if they decide to spend time on certain activities. An effective remedy for all this is surely to set up a list where to insert the various projects, putting the most important ones in the foreground (thus dividing the various propositions into two paragraphs: primary and secondary importance), writing all the projects you have in mind this moment, making sure, however, to get down to specifics being as detailed as possible. By doing this and often renewing the list, over time we will be able to stop the "windows" and restore energy. The advantages are numerous, including:

1. The proposed objectives are reached in the fastest, simplest and best way.
2. It helps to set certain tasks for the various subjects of the activity in a short period of time.
3. The most important and urgent factors are dealt with first.

If you run, however, always behind the priorities of the customers or of your collaborators, for example, and you do not use time to do the activities that if carried out regularly or in the coming months or years, will make a huge difference for your business these they will become increasingly harsh until they become real crises that will overturn any previous planning.

What are the actions that make us "waste" time unnecessarily?

● Time used to redo tasks or tasks previously performed by someone or by ourselves.

- Time used to carry out activities that are already carried out by other persons belonging to the activity.
- Time is taken to carry out superfluous/unnecessary tasks or tasks and without advantage or additional profit.
- Time wasted on revisits and unnecessary rework.

Set up the business plan

To set up a business plan, you first need to understand what a business plan is.

A business plan or "business plan" is an essential and indispensable document for a company or an activity, because it groups and explains the basics of an entire business project and has the intention of evaluating its feasibility. This allows you to take a real "picture" of the company as a whole and its own business. This project is mainly supported by a study or analysis showing an economic structure and the various planes of a company or activity.

To reach the set goal, a business plan must group all the fundamental information to:

● Understand the characteristics of the activity from which we take orientation.

● Explain the various contents of the project that will be carried out.

● Verify its implementation.

● Examine all the possible effects on the activity.

● Describe competitive forces.

● Analyze the market in which the company operates.

The business plan must, therefore, represent all the aspects of the business and then be able to evaluate its effectiveness in the reference market.

It is fundamental to keep in mind all the aspects of the extremely complex system that will be formed by the company and the world that surrounds it.

Furthermore, if we have a company history, let's use it to retrieve as much information as possible to carry out analyzes and understand how much the company will be able to grow over the years to come.

The business plan that we want to introduce is mainly based on several points, including:

- Detailed description of the business you want to use
(product study, company study, market study)
- Make the most of the available capital
(understand how much we have to spend and how to do it)
- Operational planning
(study of procurement cycle, production and logistics study, marketing plan study, study of the most suitable strategies)

- Organization of projects

(the study of the organization and the various people involved and specific roles)

To make a business plan, the following concepts must be clear.

To establish your clientele and therefore distinguish who could be really interested in your service or product, you should answer the following questions:

1. Are you referring to a specific and unique market or to several different customers?

2. Does your business identify a problem and provide an adequate solution for that situation?

3. What problem do you want to solve (or which requirement do you want to satisfy) for your customers?

4. Why should a customer choose your product or service with respect to what is already offered by the market? (example: for the quality, for the price, for the waiting time)

5. Do you have a good tool that links you and your prospective client? (How does the customer interact with your company?)

6. How do you present yourself to the market and to customers?

7. Do you have all the costs of your business under control?

Remember that you should not spend too much time perfecting your business plan. We need to think about the clientele, rather than the ideas and above all the vision, rather than the plan because to act is the last step of the ladder.

Business Manager

The Business Manager is practically a management system that allows you to manage and organize advertising accounts not only for you but also for your customers, such as Facebook, payment methods and even billing. Not only that, because the Facebook Business Manager is a platform that allows us to keep company content separate from personal content, ensuring security. In short, the Business Manager is an additional advantage that cannot be renounced.

So why should you use the Business Manager? Because it allows us to organize with greater effectiveness and security all that concerns your management activities (for a fee or not) on Facebook and Instagram and also offers us other important opportunities such as:

● It allows us to manage and organize our marketing team. Do you have an activity and do you have a marketing team that deals exclusively with social media management? In this case, the Business Manager is especially useful for organizing and entrusting certain management roles to each member of the group involved in this task.

● Through the Business Manager, we can manage multiple advertising accounts in an orderly and simple manner, thus having the opportunity to have a greater concentration of advertising in our favor.

● We can rely on external security professional. for example, if you are an activity that has commissioned your communication to an external professional, the Business Manager allows you to entrust your Facebook page, your Instagram account, etc. All this while continuing to maintain ownership of everything that belongs to you.

- With the Business Manager, we can easily assign and manage the roles of several people who work together or for you, it is, therefore, a particularly useful tool to assign to each member of the group the various roles such as editor, moderator, analyst, department head, manager of advertising, etc.

Accept failure

The fear of failure is in itself a positive feeling because it motivates us to give our best even when the ideal conditions are lacking.

This fear drives us to do much more than we usually would. Learn a lesson from failures and treasure it!

Of course, doing it is another thing: during a period of crisis you will struggle to see the positive side of the situation, but remember that it is essential for your personal growth that you can do it.

Remember that even the greatest entrepreneurs in the world have failed in their lives: just think, for example, of Steve Jobs, co-founder of Apple.

He was fired by the company he had founded, the same Apple. Then began a new adventure, founding the NeXT Computers that worked in the same sector as Apple, and with which he began to compete; Apple ended up summarizing Jobs as CEO.

Today the Apple brand has become famous thanks, above all, to its work.

Therefore, determination and passion can win in the end. The path will be full of obstacles and you will have to make incredible efforts to keep the focus, but the result will reward you for it.

No matter how much failure leads you to suffer: Steve Jobs was a human being, just like you. He found the strength to go ahead and re-launch himself in the sector he was passionate about, and he won.

The secret? Just believe it and work hard.

Tips for overcoming a failure:
Now it is clear that failure should not be seen as the end of the world, but more as a

possibility to start from scratch and not make the same mistakes.

- First of all, you need to process the incident. If a work situation goes on for years, it is not easy to find oneself starting from scratch. Take the time to think and plan with a clear mind. Analyze what went wrong and what could have been done to avoid it, to learn from the mistakes made and have an extra gear.
- We must also take responsibility, the culprit of all this is the head of the business as it is he who should make the appropriate decisions. (maybe it's also the fault of other factors, but it's too late to think about it).

Admitting your responsibilities is essential to growing from a negative situation.

- Find the positive side of failure. Think about what can be, if even small, a positive aspect of everything that is happening to you.
- Avoid making the same mistakes in the future!

If you see it the right way, failure is a great opportunity to grow and improve yourself. Moreover, it can be useful to change one's character a little, making it more motivated, determined and ready for new experiences and future failures (if they happen again).

The importance of language

English is the international language, but why is it important in the world of work?

English is the most widespread and spoken language on the Internet, so those who can understand this language can access most of the content on the Internet. Understanding all these contents is very useful when looking for information related to a certain topic, or when working or studying. English is the easiest language and is considered the most profitable investment that can be made in one's course of study. Learning to understand and speak English correctly for the world of work is essential and is above all a strategic move. English also represents many more job opportunities in Italy or abroad, in any type of company or any activity. People who know English statistically earn more On the labor market a good knowledge of English is now a very important criterion since it is considered the language of commerce, science, technology, so international trade takes place in English, articles scientific papers are written in English and all that indicates pure technology. Another fact, for example, that after Italian, English is the most used language in external and internal exchanges of the Italian business sector. In the professional world it is above all necessary to address a foreign audience, to have a sufficient level and above all to know the English vocabulary is one more step towards success.

Plan for success

Did you ever look at a successful person and envy her for her position or her earnings?

All of us, at least once in our lives, would have liked to have the knowledge and importance of another person at high levels. We must know, however, that success is built day after day and that great people are not already born, and above all, it is within the reach of everything, and it all depends on the person and the ideas one has.

How do we set up techniques to succeed? Simple, let's start with basic concepts first!

1. Our problem is actually "how" we see the problem. It is often very important to get around obstacles to overcome a certain situation or problem. There are situations that we cannot "manipulate" directly, but we can, however, find an alternative to intervene indirectly. So instead of complaining about the problem, we should try to think about what can be done alternatively. By doing this, the ability to affect the reality that surrounds us, rather than suffer it, will become ever greater.

2. Make it clear where we want to go and, therefore, be clear about the destination we are aiming for; otherwise, we will never

be able to properly plan our growth path, without following the correct direction. It is necessary, practically, to understand what really will make us happy and above all how to get there.

3. Many of the activities we do every day are urgent: we absolutely cannot postpone them to another time. What could be done to try to counteract this situation? The secret...?

Giving the right priorities to things, that is, giving priority to the most important things before they become urgent, thus avoiding arriving at the last moment with thousands of problems for the head. We must, therefore, understand how to organize ourselves during the day so as not to waste energy unnecessarily on things of little value.

4. Always be available and courteous to all those around you. For example: Respecting and understanding the priorities of the people around you, being kind and avoiding being arrogant, sincerely apologizing when you're wrong, always keeping your word (for example, a promise).

5. Avoid always putting us in the foreground, listening to the people around us is better than doing it all by yourself wrong. Most people try to always be

understood by wanting their ideas to be understood by everyone as something innovative. By doing this, we completely ignore the other person.

Being successful in life is always possible, but to do this, you have to work hard.

Brand Positioning

When we talk about positioning, we mean the method to position one's product in the minds of consumers in contrast to the products offered by the competition. For example, when we think of an expensive and luxury car, we think of a Ferrari or a Lamborghini; when we think of a work car, we think of a Volvo.

When we talk about positioning, we mean in fact, how the user distinguishes one of our products from another of the same kind, therefore, concerning the products of the competition.

Always talking about positioning a product, we refer to all those marketing techniques that aim to define the characteristics of the product and to set the appropriate marketing plan to be able to fix a certain position of our product in the mind of the consumer. The objectives are, therefore:

- Produce a product that consumers need
- Set a good value for the product and a feature that sets us apart from the competition
- Enhance your brand over competitors
- Maximize economic characteristics

So where does a positioning study want to go? Mainly aims at 3 fundamental objectives:

1. Define the strengths of each offer in part
2. Define the difference of the product or various aspects between a given subject and the competition
3. Favor the creation of "targeted" products on the target.

The positioning is therefore determined by the perception of the customers based on the proposed product, and to make it effective, the product that we have proposed on the market must be memorized and remembered by the customers, in fact to position the new product better than the other competitors we should look for to fill empty spaces in consumers' minds. The fundamental questions to which we must answer before carrying out a positioning study are:

➔ Are other companies or other competitors already implementing a positioning study like ours?

➔ The study we're going to do, is it so profitable to attract new customers?

→ Is the product we are proposing able to keep the promises we made before the customer makes the purchase?

The positioning strategies are:
- Superiority against competitors, being better, being innovative.
- Explain the needs that our product can meet and if it has characteristics.
- Based on the category our product belongs to
- In contrast to a certain product that already exists on the market

Getting the customer to desire you

To be desired by the customer means to be appreciated and above all to give a good impression. Before understanding how to "conquer" a customer, you need to have an answer to these questions:

- What is their need so they should buy from you?
- What do they need?
- Why should they buy from you?
- Do you offer the right solution to their needs?

Getting a good reputation among your customers is not always so obvious and easy, as this factor can be crucial to determine the success of an activity and above all the rate of purchases. To better understand the concept, just think of an ordinary product: For example, when we think of sports shoes, the first thing that comes to mind is the Nike brand, Adidas or other successful companies that manufacture quality products. Well, the same thing must also happen in this sector, when the customer thinks about the product or service he needs, he must immediately think of us and the excellent comfort we give to the customer!

Were you able to win over your customers? Perfect, after you've arrived at this point, you simply have to continue to "travel" them, through purchase proposals through and promotions and offers, making sure that the customer has the perception that you are constantly present and that you don't want to lose it.

In this way you will be able to retain customers, obtaining two very important advantages: not only will the customers who have already purchased continue to do so, but they will also begin to talk about you with their network, thus bringing you other customers.

What is the key to making customers loyal, and having the certainty that they will return to you in the future?

You have to make them feel important and build a relationship, even a personal one, that lasts over time.

The simplest and most effective way to do this is to understand the needs of the individual customer and offer a personalized service.

Another technique is to submit surveys and questionnaires to customers. Asking them for their personal opinion, making them feel valued and making them perceive this as your interest in them and towards their personal concepts. Thus establishing an emotional relationship that lasts over time: in this regard, social networks will be of great help: in a short time and with little effort you will be able to communicate, on a personal level, with hundreds, if not thousands of customers.

The Social Networks also offers the possibility to talk to those who follow us, in this way it is possible to dialogue with their customers even from a distance and in any situation. By doing so, customers will have the feeling of being very close to you by actively participating in your business. Once you are familiar with and learn to make the best use of Social Networks, you can get a huge advantage from these, such as: setting up a relationship that does not fade over time between you and the customer. Also important in this situation is the so-called "Social Monitoring" activity, which is an activity that takes care of observing, monitoring, listening and reporting the various behaviors of customers, their daily habits, their needs, their expectations and above all of their desires. By knowing our customers, we are able to understand what kind of content they want us to present to them, which will allow us to set up our marketing offer in order to retain them.

Create your own reputation

Reputation is the result of a long journey that your business has exposed to the public, reputation, but it is always at risk.

It is the result of hard work to strengthen its image to an external public, built by an organization or a single subject whose main task is to interact positively and actively with external people.

Always at risk, why? Simple, just quote a sentence from a famous successful man; "It takes 20 years to build a reputation, but it takes 5 minutes to ruin it."

The reputation of a person or an activity, therefore, is a communicative product derived from the relationship between the organization and its customers. Customers are therefore in some way fixing the concept of reputation, so I am able both to create it and destroy it. Reputation can also be an important competitive advantage, and therefore, an additional tool against the competition.

Reputation depends on how other people see us, how we look in the eyes of customers and all other people. A good reputation can be advantageous against the competition and is a means that allows us to know and receive new customers, but also to retain customers who may not yet have total confidence, or simply those who want to know us better and are waiting. Reputation is divided into several paragraphs, including:

1. Your own style (everyone can build a reputation in their own way).

2. The way to relate (how we behave and how we relate to new people or stable customers).

3. Actual behavior.

Promote your product

The first step for the promotion of a product is the identification of the target audience, that is the people we want to address.

To sell effectively, it is essential to know your model buyer in all its details. Focusing on the whole population is not, in fact, an effective choice: our advertising budget will be spread over so many people that it will not have any effect, and the communication will be anonymous and without ideas.

So it all depends on the type of product we intend to promote: your target can be composed, for example, by men, women, children, etc.

The first step is, therefore, to learn to target the public that will most likely be interested in our proposal: the better we succeed in this task, the more effective our communication efforts will be.

The advice is, therefore, to start with a very narrow slice, the so-called laser target, to eventually expand the audience at a later date.

But how can we promote a product?

Now we know the ideal target and we are in the right direction.

Now we need to find a way to better promote the product.

The first element of a successful sales plan are the goals we set ourselves before implementing it all; to decide we must aim high, hoping to get there.

Think, for example, how many units of the product you want and are able to sell the first month.

Once this is done, we must think about what sales techniques you are going to adopt, for example: who will address the customer? An abstract person or company? Will you communicate through the website or a physical store?

All this must be defined in what the sales plan is. Another factor to consider is the temporal factor: how long do you expect to achieve the result you want and how much are you willing to work or invest to succeed?

This type of planning is really fundamental: you won't need anything to create slogans and advertising initiatives unless you have first of all defined the objective of these operations.

The first thing to do is to evaluate if the product you have proposed to the public has value for the customers you have decided to bet on, to understand if they are interested if it's worth it. Represents an innovation, something that when you see it, you can't help it?

To arrive in the hands of the customer, now, our product must also be able to attract the attention of the public.

Even the eye wants its part: just think of a product that can easily succeed in a randomly made packaging; everything can be safely thrown away since it is a game lost at the start.

The promotional message that we are going to choose and put on the packaging must be clear, simple and above all direct: with just one look, the customer must be able to understand what is present inside, how and what the product we are proposing can be useful for; in short, it must go and hit straight to the point.

Just think that today's consumers only tend to buy a product that they know they need, quickly and easily.

The basis is still the need: the product must be useful and solve a problem for people.

However, even respecting these rules, it is almost impossible that the product you are offering on the market is the only one of its kind and that you have no competitor who has produced and had the same idea: you must, therefore, be able to communicate with customers in so as to highlight the advantages of your product compared to the competition.

It must be understood, however, that there is no product without defects and yours is included in this category. The thing to do is to understand what the problems are and try to eliminate them so that it is not the consumer who realizes it and go on to affect your reputation.

Just think that even the most innovative product of all can become a total fiasco if it is not proposed and presented to the public in an appropriate and just way.

Not only must the customer be willing to accept the defects of your product, which will be inevitable: it must also be willing to pay the amount requested.

Where would you start your sales business from?

Simple, you could, for example, use your site where you sell your products, like eBay, for example. Or, as we have seen, you can use social networks, perhaps organizing local events to which invite friends and their friends.

Finally from the first feedback, you will receive from your customers, you will be able to understand where to improve!

To be able to promote and above all sell a certain product, it is very important to be found by customers.

Such as? With the creation of a website, through advertisements in appropriate situations.

It would be convenient to be easily findable through the common words sought by your potential customers every day on Google. Careful though: SEO is an extremely complex field and being the first for words that no one is looking for will not be of much help to you.

Pricing

Have you ever wondered if the price you want to sell your product is effective?

Now let's see how to decide the price of a product that we want to put on the market, starting from the base, the price is determined by finding the various expenses that I found in production (including work) and adding the sum of money I would like to earn; in simpler words "How much did I spend to make that particular product?"

To evaluate a price, we often turn to the market, looking at the prices offered by the competition, whether they are high, medium or low. But this is not always the best solution, some think that if I sell at a price higher than the competition or at the variable price that is on the market, I am doomed to failure; absolutely not!

In fact, the price in most cases is determined by the customer's expectations, greater expectations will satisfy and consequently the higher the price we could offer; surely a quality product will cost much more than a low-quality one, just think about the workmanship behind it, or the number of expectations it satisfies.

This is not always the case, since the price is the seller who decides it and not the market, the competition or any other subject outside his business.

Maybe you have used technologies that have come to cost you more for the realization of a product, maybe you have used a valuable material because you should choose a price of a similar product that has the same task of satisfying the same need, similar to what?

Maybe he has lower production costs, so he chose a price based on that; and this is why we have to choose it, without depending on others.

It must be said, however, that there are some cases where a good quality product is cheap, in fact, the number of sales is certainly higher than a poor quality product at the same price.

The price of a product can also be determined by the need and need to have that particular product at a specific time, for example: It is winter, outside there are 5 ° and we have an important appointment that we absolutely cannot miss, the problem however it's that it's too cold to go out without a jacket to shelter us from the cold; here, in this case, the need to own a jacket is certainly greater than the need to possess any other good at that precise moment.

The price of the jacket can be subject to variations at a specific time of the year, since it is a product that at a given moment has greater importance than a shirt, rather than a bathing suit, for example.

It is enough to understand that since I need a product at that moment, I am willing to spend even more.

Just think: we are in the desert, and we are 40 °, we have not been drinking for 2 days, a bottle of water that may be at this moment in our house is worth nothing, or very little, what value would it have in that situation? You would be willing to spend even hundreds if not thousands for a glass of water.

It is very important to understand when to propose our product, and when to raise and lower prices.

Know your customer

Knowing the client we are addressing means understanding what he needs, what his main goals are, and if he has other needs that we can satisfy, and understand why he has taken certain actions. It is also very important to understand the characteristics of the customer, what kind of person we are addressing, who we are on the other side of the screen. We must, therefore, understand what the customer wants and why he turned to us.

Understanding the customer means interpreting how the study we are proposing can be profitable, and if it can be useful during his journey. In this way, we will be able to relate better with the customer we are facing.

Once established a relationship like this, the price we are proposing will be seen with different eyes, as a fact of second importance, in fact, the customer will give him less importance than usual. Knowing the customer we are addressing means, therefore:

• Establish a good relationship, not only of trust, which lasts over time.

• Try to make the price as a secondary, less important aspect

- Make the customer understand that we are the perfect solution to their problems.
- Keep customers, to make them see the competition as a disadvantage.
- Customer loyalty and increase profits.
- Better relationship between all your staff and customers.

To know the customer we are addressing, what are his needs, his needs, how much he wants to spend if it is right for us: we can ask him direct questions in order to make them feel important and in the foreground.

The results we will obtain will be better and more precise if our study is carried out in a well structured and organized way.

We basically have to listen to them, nothing more for now: we must understand that customers often like to give long and detailed answers because they want to expose their plans, ideas and above all their needs and how you could be useful to them. The approach can be of various types, through surveys, for example; or you can simply talk to us directly through a conversation that can take place online or physically from which you can get information to understand and learn more about the client and his needs.

Many people ask themselves, even if the customer trusts us and knows us now, why don't they pay?

The reasons why a customer decides are not paid are many, now we will analyze some of them:

1. The customer does not yet feel like buying, maybe he wants to wait and get to know us better, better understand our plans and our proposals. To do this it is we who must accompany him on this journey

and make them understand all our intentions.

2. The customer is disorganized, perhaps economically, or he simply forgot to pay off a debt.

4. The client cannot pay off the debt because he has financial problems. Another factor that determines why the customer does not pay, is because perhaps our offer has a fairly substantial cost and the customer does not have the economic possibility to pay us at that precise moment and therefore, even if he has every intention of buying, he will not since it does

not have the amount of money requested by us.

5. The customer refuses to pay. The right thing to do is to pay first and then offer the product or service that we are proposing, to prevent the customer from taking advantage of it and refusing to pay in the future.

Errors to avoid

Differentiate prices

One of the biggest mistakes that can be made is to differentiate the prices of the service offered for each customer, knowing that one may have more money than the other.

One of the reasons why people are rich is certainly because they are better at handling and investing money than you.

An account is when the customer chooses the package he wants to use (example: business class) chosen by him, another account is instead when there is a single package available, in this case, a single service, and since he has I pay a lot more money.

The concept to understand is one: equal prices for all, if one has more money it does not mean that he has to pay more, or vice versa.

We must know that the truth sooner or later comes to the surface if we break this pillar because people are not stupid and they realize that we are robbing them. Just think of the situation that would form: "A customer buys a specific service for the price of € 500, another that has more money spends € 800 for the same service, after a few days the customer with more money realizes what happened ", And it is here that a real situation of confusion is created by both parties and above all among all customers. What would you say to the customer who comes to you saying "Why did you charge me more and instead to him less?" It would be a huge blow to reputation, which would make you dishonest, leading you to failure.

Another factor to absolutely avoid, are the so-called "hidden costs," when you have to have your client pay a certain amount of money, be straightforward and clear, saying all you have to pay immediately, not in a few months calling him and telling him "look that you have to pay another 600 €" absolutely to be avoided.

Discounts

What would you say if a customer asks you to give him a discount?

Surely it is a question that puts most marketers in crisis; some trying to answer with a joke, those who try to justify themselves with quality but almost all of them give in and start to lower the price, believing that it is the only way not to lose the customer, on the other hand, it is an absolutely stupid thing to do.

Perhaps they will not lose the customer, but the only one who earns from this situation is the customer.

Selling a series of products in the same niche, with even lower gains than those belonging to different niches, but creating a brand, giving value to time and being very careful with every single detail.

This means that if one of your customers buys your product and is comfortable with it, he can decide to buy another product that you sell in the same niche under the same brand, it's called cross-selling.

To make money online you never leave the product, but the customer!

If there is a question then you have to offer the answer to your request and turn that question into a sale. Those who first look at the product and then at the customer target make a big mistake.

Try to think of having a beautiful, super functional product that nobody cares about, what would you do with it? The important thing for those who are starting to sell online is to look for their target among millions of people who are there to listen to you and are ready to spend their money. How to find the right customer? Everything starts with a very specific question: "Who is my client? Why should he buy from me and not from others? Yes, they are two questions but they are closely connected.

Finding the right customer is the starting point to create a Funnel or a winning online marketing strategy. Try to think of how many people put their data on social networks ... There is nothing left but to put on paper the identikit of our best customer and that's it! When you go to create a marketing campaign through Facebook, for example, you can select age, sex, preferences, cities and interests! Here everything is played: if I am not able to bring the interested customer into my path, I will not only lose money but I will probably not get any results.

Below I want to list a series of strategic answers with which you can respond to the request for discount set by the customer and come out 100% winning: you have to present yourself decisively with pride for your company, try to find out as much information as possible about the customer that you have to face, you must understand his needs in order to have useful information for the negotiation; when you present your products you must give great importance to the service offered and highlighting the various aspects that differentiate you from your competitors, you must absolutely defend yourself from discount requests and make them believe that the prices indicated are not changeable but are fixed and are pre-established by a superior.

Always remember a basic rule that I told you a little earlier: always try to collect your customers' data, they are essential for marketing online!

I will now show you an example of a Funnel-based strategy that will allow you to create an effective sales page in just a few steps!

Don't worry if you think you don't know how to create an automated route or an online platform, in the final chapter I'll explain you a few tricks to speed things up, start with a marketing campaign on Facebook or Adwords or more simply by traffic! In short, it doesn't matter if you use one tool rather than another, the important thing is to use the one that fits your audience and get the result!

We must bring all our visitors directly to an Opt-in data acquisition system. The Opt-in is a page, or mini-website of a single page, which collects and shows visitors a very precise message about our product or service, or about what they want to get. In this page, we have to insert the exact bait that allows us to capture the email and the name of our user transforming it into a Lead (a qualified contact). As you can see, the scheme is very intuitive and simple and shows you that, once you leave the email, the customer will have to receive the link to the bait via email and above all, he must automatically switch to the second level of our Funnel.

If we are selling an affiliate product, the second level can usually be directly the product sales page or an intermediate page containing additional information designed to increase the value of the product. If you pay attention you will see that, as soon as a customer leaves his email, a series of 5 specific emails will be sent, day after day.

This phase, called Nurturing, is necessary to increase the conversion rate without spending an extra Euro. Indeed, once collecting the email, the customer becomes ours and we do not need to pay to show our offer or to contact the customer, just a very simple email. Obviously, it must be sent automatically! I will explain later how to put into practice what I have just explained to you, for now, don't worry, just try to understand the strategy. If instead, you wanted to sell your product, this path could have a specific order page for the product as the second level.

Do you need money?

Another strategy that can make you dodge if studied and applied correctly is to be able to make the customer perceive "a lack of interest from you" in selling this product; why are you wondering?

Trust that this is a winning strategy, let me give you some examples, if a customer perceives your pressure that you are desperately trying to sell him something then he is very likely to choose not to buy; if, on the other hand, you present the product to the same customer in the best way but without mentioning the following: are you interested in buying? or: I advise you to hurry to buy; then the customer will feel free to choose and will, of course, feel the urgency to buy and most likely he will tell you that he wants

conclude the purchase.

Having said that, it may seem strange to you if you are not very experienced, yet I can guarantee that it is so, before proceeding to sell your product through a marketing strategy you must be clear about things, you must have an answer to all these questions: who is my ideal client? Where can I find it? How much does it cost me to find it? How can I make my products interested? What result do I want to get?

This is the real secret formula for every successful funnel!

Analyze and plan well before proceeding to the most interesting part of funnel marketing! Now he will explain the questions I asked you earlier, let's start with the first one:

- Who is our ideal client?

Have you ever asked yourself this question? Many think that all of them are their ideal customers, but they are not! There are only 100 real fans. Have you ever heard of it? 100 real fans produce 80% of your turnover! See, I'm their people who do not dedicate their time to everyone, but only to those who offer their product of interest, this is the goal to reach high levels in online marketing and be able to place themselves in every sector with success!

- Where can I find it?

Analyzing where we can find our possible customer is the other step that allows us not to waste money unnecessarily and without obtaining appreciable results.

- How can I make my products interested?

We continue analyzing my business idea and which bait to use to capture my possible client.

- What result do I want to achieve?

Before starting any operation I advise you to play a little game: take a blank sheet and draw your possible customer, then draw the route you would like him to do and how much you would like him to spend. Only to this dot you will understand the bait to use and where to find your client, I read more and more often, for example in the affiliations,

marketing operations with a very unprofitable result: no means to collect customer data and above all no bait! Sometimes I see online or on social posts of people selling products in affiliation, without even knowing what it means to do affiliation and above all without knowing how to do online marketing, which is more serious. Before proceeding and understanding how to put a business online and how to find new customers through a Funnel, I want to explain to you the economic cycle of a product. Many tend not to understand this type of mechanism that shows you if you are making gains rather than losses! It seems absurd, but most people throw away a lot of money online precisely because they believe it is easier to sell cheap products. This is true, but here we are talking about making money online and not doing favors. Try to imagine this scene, which is what you see most often on Facebook:

Affiliate product: € 29

Earnings from the sale: € 10.

www.ingramcontent.com/pod-product-compliance
Lightning Source LLC
Chambersburg PA
CBHW070421220526
45466CB00004B/1495